SQUEALS
&
SQUIGGLES
&
GHOSTLY GIGGLES

FOUR WINDS PRESS   NEW YORK

SQUEALS & SQUIGGLES & GHOSTLY GIGGLES

by Ann McGovern

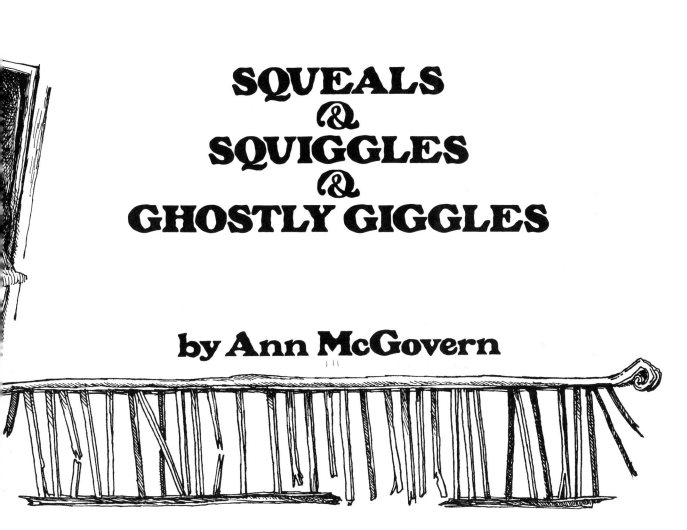

illustrated by Jeffrey Higginbottom

PUBLISHED BY FOUR WINDS PRESS.

A DIVISION OF SCHOLASTIC MAGAZINES, INC., NEW YORK, N.Y.

TEXT COPYRIGHT © 1973 BY ANN MCGOVERN.

ILLUSTRATIONS COPYRIGHT © 1973 BY JEFFREY HIGGINBOTTOM.

ALL RIGHTS RESERVED.

PRINTED IN THE UNITED STATES OF AMERICA.

LIBRARY OF CONGRESS CATALOGUE CARD NUMBER: 72-87083

1 2 3 4 5 77 76 75 74 73

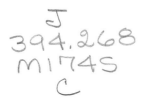

CONTENTS

For my favorite Jaimes

LIMER-EEKS

There once was a demon as green
As any there ever had been.
 He would hide in the grass
 To watch people pass,
Convinced that he couldn't be seen.

A ghoul dug a grave six feet deep
And climbed in, preparing to sleep.
 But he heard someone sneeze,
 And, though weak in the knees,
He bounded back out in one leap.

It's said there are spooks who find fun,
In undoing things that are done.
    They go to foot races
    And untie shoelaces,
Then watch people trip as they run.

A goblin who lived on the moon
Decided he'd have to leave soon
    To avoid being caught
    By the strange astronaut
Who was coming the next day at noon.

Tonight, when the last light is gone
And you're almost too sleepy to yawn,
    Put your ear to the wall
    And you'll hear the Thing crawl,
But don't cry; it leaves before dawn.

There once was a pale apparition,
Who suffered from grave malnutrition.
    Said Mom, "If you don't eat your toast,
    You'll soon be a ghost."
    Said he, "That's just superstition!"

3

A zombie who thought he was dying
Just could not seem to stop crying
    Until his friend said,
    "You're already quite dead,"
So the zombie's tears began drying.

A ghost who had lost his head
Got up on the wrong side of bed.
    He had to go haunting
    But his head he was wanting
So he took his friend's head instead.

On a cold wintry night in a blizzard
A skeleton dined with a wizard.
    The tea room they rode to
    Was fresh out of toad stew,
So they had to eat finely ground lizard.

A skeleton known as Jack Sprat
Can no longer sit where he sat.
    For when he was thin,
    He could sit on a pin,
But now he is getting too fat.

A werewolf named Wendy is fair,
So long as the sun is up there.
    But, when the moon rises,
    She puts on disguises—
With fangs and a lot of coarse hair.

Wanda Witch decided to see
How the wizards made their tea.
    They boiled some bats
    And some tails from rats
Then gave her a cup for free.

Slimey Spook hates his name,
And his friends all feel the same.
If you were Slimey, wouldn't you
Rather be called another name, too?

A vampire who rarely vacations
Planned to visit a number of nations.
    When told with regrets
    That he couldn't bring pets,
He replied, "But my bats are relations!"

Greta Gremlin, evil thing.
How does your garden grow?
   With unrhymed poems,
   Twelve three-eyed gnomes,
And one ghoul six feet below.

A ghoul and his girl, for a lark,
Went strolling one night in the park.
   They stopped under a light,
   And the ghoul cried in fright,
"EEK! Quick dear, get back in the dark!"

A ghost, who had once been afraid,
To play games that the other ghosts played,
   Found by just saying, "BOO!"
   He could be scary, too.
And thus his whole future was made.

A witch who was ugly as sin
Went to work at the Pirate Inn.
   She would sweep up the rooms
   With her long-handled brooms,
And frighten the guests with her grin.

GAMES

FEEL THE CORPSE

Tell your friends they are going to be "in touch" with a corpse!
But don't tell them the grisly parts are really . . .

   broken pretzels~for teeth
   two freshly peeled onions~for eyes
   two dried apricots~for ears
   chalk~for fingers
   mop head~for hair
   pork and beans~for insides
   carrot~for nose
   wet sponge~for brains

   Put these items on a tray and put a sheet over yourself for a
ghost costume. Darken the room and tell your friends to sit
around a table. Give them each a towel to cover their laps.
   As each part of the corpse is mentioned, pass it around the

7

table for your friends to feel. In your spookiest voice, read this poem:

If you must hold these, please don't fumble,
For if you do, my teeth will crumble.   (*pretzels*)

Ah, here are my long-lost eyes.
Hold them to your nose—surprise!   (*onions*)

Have you ever tasted ears,
Buried for a thousand years?   (*dried apricots*)

Oh, how rigor mortis lingers
In my dry and bony fingers!   (*chalk*)

Now my skull is cold and bare,
For in your hands you hold my hair!   (*mop head*)

Oh woe is me, oh woe betide me—
This gloppy goo was once inside me!   (*pork and beans*)

Listen my friends, listen my foes.
You can't smell good without a nose.   (*carrot*)

Don't scream, don't faint and don't complain,
You have me all, for here's my brain!   (*wet sponge*)

(Exit with a ghostly cry, while your friends shiver.)

8

OUTWITTING THE WITCH

Do you want to stage a terrorizing treasure hunt? Change your name to Wilmer (or Wilma) Wizard and outwit a wicked witch!

Read the following message to your friends (or make up your own):

YOU HAVE BEEN PUT UNDER THE EVIL SPELL OF A WICKED WITCH. YOU WILL BE TURNED INTO MICE AT MIDNIGHT UNLESS YOU CAN FIND THE CHARMS TO OUTWIT THE WITCH AND TURN HER INTO CHEWING GUM!

W. WIZARD

Before the treasure hunt begins, collect the magic charms for outwitting the witch. Read the following three pages to learn where to hide them. And then ask a few friends to your house for some spooky fun!

You'll need:

a four-leaf clover (If you can't find one, draw one—it's just as lucky.)

a rabbit's foot (You can draw a rabbit's foot, too, if you have trouble catching a rabbit.)

bat's hair (a ball of wool or yarn)

toad's eyes (marbles or pebbles)

vampire's blood (a glass of tomato juice)

With each magic charm, place the clue for the charm you want your friends to find next. The first person to find the charm should wait until everyone has reached the spot. Then the next clue is read and everyone rushes off to look for the charm it describes.

Here's the first clue!

TURN FOUR LEAVES OF A SCIENCE BOOK
TO FIND WHAT WITCHES OVERLOOK.

Hide the four-leaf clover between pages 8 and 9 of your science book. Leave the book in plain sight on a table or chair. With the four-leaf clover, your friends will find the next clue:

WITH A LITTLE LUCK, I HOPE
YOU'LL FIND TOAD'S EYES. GO WASH WITH SOAP!

Put marbles or pebbles in the bathroom soap dish, with the next clue:

FIND THE SHOE IN WHICH I'VE PUT
A CHARM AND YOU'LL FIND LUCK AFOOT.
ONCE YOU'VE FOUND IT, BETTER GRAB IT,
OR YOU'LL LOSE IT TO A RABBIT.

Put the rabbit's foot in a shoe and hide it under the sofa. With the rabbit's foot, leave the next clue:

WHEN THE MOON IS BRIGHT AND FULL,
THE HAIR OF BATS IS MUCH LIKE WOOL,
IF YOU WOULD BE SAFE FROM HARM,
THE HAIR OF BATS MUST BE YOUR CHARM.
DON'T LOOK UP: LOOK DOWN INSTEAD,
UPON THE PLACE I LAY MY HEAD!

12

Put the wool on your pillow with the next clue:

WHEN IT'S CHILLED AND GETS QUITE COLD,
VAMPIRE'S BLOOD IS VERY NICE.
YOUR FINAL CLUE I'LL HERE UNFOLD.
YOU'LL FIND HIS BLOOD WHERE YOU FIND ICE.

Put glass of tomato juice and the next message from W. Wizard
in the freezer of the refrigerator.

When everyone has reached the kitchen, read W. Wizard's message aloud.

YOU'VE FOUND THE CHARMS;
YOU'VE SOLVED THE CLUES.
THE WICKED WITCH KNOWS SHE MUST LOSE.
YOU'VE HEEDED WELL
MY GOOD ADVICE.
YOU'LL NOT BE TURNED TO LITTLE MICE.
WITH FOUR-LEAF CLOVER,
RABBIT'S FOOT,
A HEX UPON THE WITCH YOU'VE PUT.
ADD HAIR OF BAT
AND TOAD'S BRIGHT EYES.
THE WITCH IS IN FOR A SURPRISE.
ADD VAMPIRE'S BLOOD,
AND NOW YOU'RE DONE.
THE BATTLE WITH THE WITCH IS WON.

THE WIZARD'S WISE,
THE WITCH IS DUMB,
FOR LOOK WHAT SHE HAS NOW BECOME . . .
CHEWING GUM!

Give each of your friends a stick of gum.

THE FOUR WITCHES

HERE'S THE TRICK

Tell your friend there are four witches hidden in a deck of cards. His job: to find them.

Ask him to divide the deck into four piles and put them on the table as the picture shows.

He picks up the first pile. He takes three cards from the first pile and puts them down. He deals one card from the first pile onto each of the other three piles. Then he puts the remaining cards from the first pile on top of the three cards.

He picks up the second pile. He takes three cards from the second pile and puts them down. He deals one card from the second pile onto each of the other three piles. Then he replaces the cards from the second pile on top of the three cards.

He does the same thing with the third and fourth piles.

By this time, it looks as if the cards are thoroughly mixed up. So your friend will be doubly amazed when he turns up the top card on each pile—and uncovers the four witches (queens)!

 15

HERE'S HOW

Before you amaze your friend, do this: put the four queens on top of the deck. When your friend divides the deck into four piles, be sure that the pile with the four queens is the fourth pile.

Practice this trick alone before you mystify your friends with it.

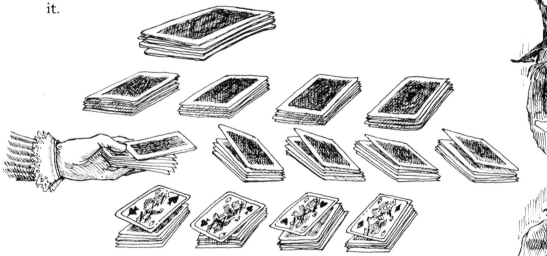

From first pile, deal off three cards, then deal one card onto each of the other three piles, then replace pile on the first three cards dealt from it. Do the same with second, third, and fourth piles.

Turn up top card of each pile. *There are the four witches!*

16

THE SKELETON'S BONES

You probably know dominoes as a game to play. But for this trick, you tell a friend that the dominoes are the "bones" of a pirate who was forced to walk the plank. Why? He gave away too many secrets. And now the pirate is a skeleton, but he is still telling secrets.

Tell your friend to mix up the "bones" or dominoes. Ask him to arrange the bones in one continuous line, as the drawing shows, matching end to end.

As he is doing this, say: "The skeleton has told me a secret number." Write down the number, fold the paper, and put it aside.

When your friend has finished arranging the bones of the skeleton, ask him to open the folded paper. Say, "Abracadabra! The skeleton has given away another secret."

The numbers you wrote are the same numbers that are on either end of the line of "bones."

You can repeat this trick right away and as often as you wish, using a different pair of secret numbers each time.

17

HERE'S HOW

Before your friend begins to arrange the dominoes, take one and hide it in your pocket. Be sure it has two different numbers. The two numbers on this domino are the numbers you write down.

If you repeat the trick, exchange the domino that you first hid for a new one with two different numbers and write these two numbers down.

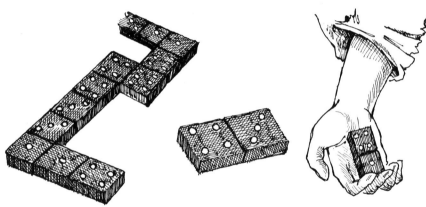

Your friend joins dominoes into a single chain, matching end to end as in the game. The two numbers at the end of chain match your prediction.

To make prediction, write down the two numbers from the domino which you have hidden. The numbers on it will be the numbers at the end of chain.

THE BEWITCHED BAND

HERE'S THE TRICK

Say to a friend, "I hold in my hand a 3,000-year-old headband found on a skeleton. It seems to be bewitched."

Tell your friend to cut the band the long way. Much to his surprise he will find he has one long band, not two!

"Aha," you say. "This band is certainly bewitched. Let's try again."

Ask your friend to cut the band the long way again. This time, he will end up with two bands, but they will be mysteriously linked together!

To make the band, take a strip of paper about one inch wide and twelve inches long. Before gluing the ends together, give one end a half-turn twist, as the drawing shows.

Give strip half twist
before gluing ends together.

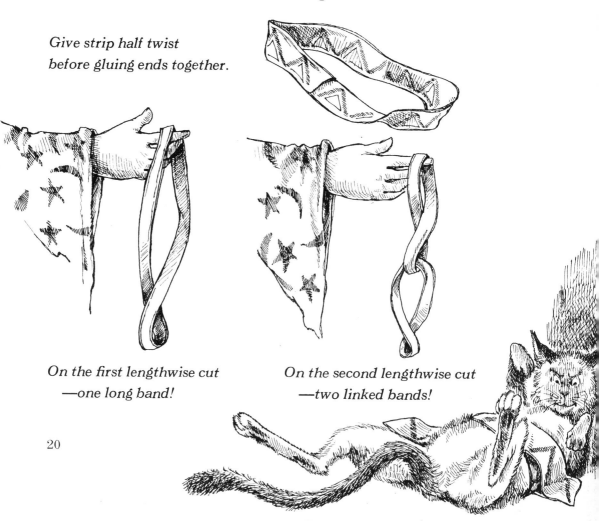

On the first lengthwise cut
    —one long band!

On the second lengthwise cut
    —two linked bands!

20

THE PAST AND THE FUTURE: FUNTASTIC FORTUNES

You don't need a crystal ball to tell fortunes. All you need is a deck of cards.

Ask a friend to shuffle the cards. Then lay out seven cards, face up in a row. These cards reveal the past.

Lay out a second row of seven cards. These cards foretell the future.

Study the chart to learn what each card represents. Until you become an expert fortune-teller, you'll probably want to keep the chart handy.

Try telling your own fortune first to get the hang of it.

SPADES	HEARTS	DIAMONDS	CLUBS
School	Family or Friends	Money	Sports or Hobbies

KING: father
QUEEN: mother
JACK: teacher
TEN: find something
NINE: lose something
EIGHT: long journey

SEVEN: short trip
SIX: surprising news
FIVE: fight
FOUR: good luck
THREE: bad luck
TWO: love
ACE: health

Suppose the seven cards that foretell the future turn out to be: King of spades, ten of spades, nine of hearts, three of diamonds, eight of clubs, five of hearts, and the Jack of diamonds . . .

22

The King of spades tells you that your father will be asked to school. (That could be either good or bad.) The ten of spades means you will find something in school. (Your father?) The nine of hearts means that your best friend will lose something of yours. (Your report card?) The eight of clubs means you will take a long journey having to do with one of your hobbies. The three of diamonds means you will have bad luck with money. (You might lose a dime on your long journey.) And the five of hearts means a fight with your sister or brother. The Jack of diamonds has something to do with money and your teacher. (Perhaps your teacher will suddenly become a millionairess, or she might ask you to bring some money to school for a class treat.)

When you tell your friend's fortune, keep it fun. Fortune telling is only for fun.

THE WITCH'S TEETH

HERE'S THE TRICK

Show three dice to a friend. Tell him they were once the teeth of a witch and still have magic powers.

Turn your back. Tell your friend to roll the dice and to add up the numbers showing on the tops of the three dice.

Then tell him to pick one up and to add the number on the bottom of it to his previous total.

Tell him to roll this one again. This time he adds the number showing on the top to his total.

Now turn around. Pick up the dice and hold them to your forehead. Then say: "The dice feel cold and clammy. The witch is using her power to tell me the answer." After a moment of looking mysterious, announce the correct figure.

24

Before you pick up the dice, add the numbers showing on the tops of all three. Then add seven to your total for your answer. This trick works all the time!

Your friend rolls three dice and adds the numbers shown on their top faces. Then he picks up one die and adds the number

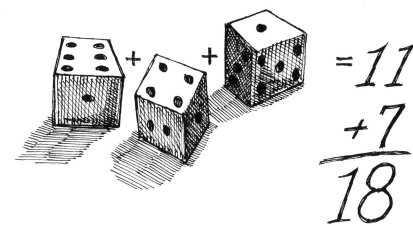

$$= 11$$
$$+ 7$$
$$\overline{18}$$

showing on its bottom face. Then he rolls this die once again and adds the number on its top face for a grand total. You turn around and with a little hocus-pocus announce correctly the total he reached. (Just add seven to the total showing on the three top faces.)

THE GALLOPING GHOST

Say to a friend, "There's a galloping ghost who lives in the pockets of my pants. He gallops from one pocket to another."

Pull out the two front pockets of your pants to prove to your friend they are empty. Put the pockets back in. Then hold out your hands to show your friend that they are empty, too.

Pick up a white handkerchief and say, "This is the galloping ghost. Watch him carefully."

Put the handkerchief into your right-hand pocket. Pull the pocket out again. It's empty—"no ghost"! Push the pocket back in.

Reach into your left pocket—and out comes the "ghost." Put the "ghost" back into your left pocket, and show your friends your hands are empty. Reach into your left pocket and pull it out again. This time it's empty.

Reach into your right pocket and pull out the "ghost." Push both of your pockets back in. Then place the "ghost" in your right pocket.

Snap your fingers, say, "Glibety-glabbity-glanished." And, wonder of wonders, the "ghost" has vanished!

26

HERE'S HOW

Make sure you're wearing pants with pockets that can be pulled out. You'll need two small white handkerchiefs or cloths that look alike. In the inside upper corner of each of your pockets is a small space in which you can hide a tightly folded handkerchief which will remain hidden even when you pull out your pockets.

Before you begin the trick, tightly fold a handkerchief and hide it in the corner of your left pocket. As you do the trick, simply wad up the handkerchief and tuck it into the corner of the pocket from which you want the "ghost" to disappear. Then reach into the other pocket and produce the "ghost," holding it between two fingers so that it unfolds. At the end of the trick, leave one handkerchief tightly folded in the corner of each pocket.

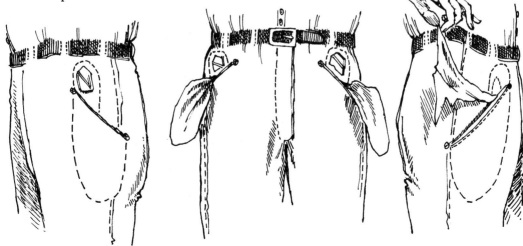

THE UNHANGABLE HOBGOBLIN

HERE'S THE TRICK

Tell your friends this story of Jorge (say Hor-gay) the Unhangable Hobgoblin:

A hobgoblin by the name of Jorge was sentenced to be hanged for playing tricks on the king. When Jorge learned that he would die by hanging, he only smiled and said, "I'm Jorge, the Unhangable Hobgoblin."

On the day of his execution, Jorge was still smiling and saying over and over: "I'm Jorge, the Unhangable Hobgoblin."

Even as the noose was placed over his neck and the ropes were tightening around his neck, Jorge was saying, "I'm Jorge, the Unhangable Hobgoblin." And sure enough—the ropes passed right through Jorge's neck. He jumped to the ground unharmed, and ran safely out of the kingdom.

Tell your friends that Jorge has passed his magic secret to you and that you will demonstrate that a rope can pass through your waist as easily as it passed through Jorge's neck.

28

Hold up two cords, six feet long or longer. Pass the cords behind your back and bring the ends around in front of you. Tie an overhand knot in two of the ends, and tell two friends to stand on either side of you and to grasp the cords. Tell them to chant, "Jorge, the Unhangable Hobgoblin," while you count to ten.

On the count of ten, your friends are to tug firmly on the cords. Lo and behold! They pass right through your waist!

You can make this trick more mysterious by pretending to grow nervous as you count toward ten.

When you first show the cords, it looks as if you are holding them side by side. But actually, hidden in your hand, the two cords are doubled and joined together only by a loop of thread —just strong enough to hold until the cords are pulled taut. Stand with your back to the wall or wear a jacket, your shirt outside your pants, so your friends won't be able to see the loops or the thread behind your back. When they pull on the cords, the thread breaks and it looks as if the cord has passed right through you!

Your audience thinks it sees two ropes, side by side.
Actually, the ropes are doubled and held together by a loop of thread.

Put the ropes behind your back, leaving them doubled. Then bring the ends around in front of you. Take one end from each side and tie a knot that joins them in front of you. Tell two friends to each take one of the loose ends that are left. When they tug, the ropes pass through you.

THE DISAPPEARING DEMON

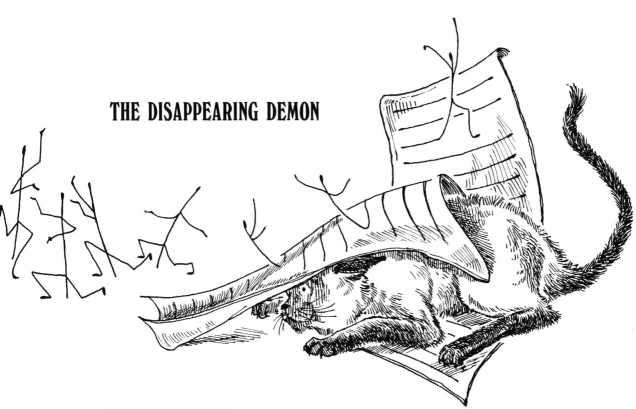

HERE'S THE TRICK

Show a friend two pieces of paper fitted together as in the first picture below and tell him that the ten lines represent ten demons. The demons have been making too much mischief and everyone is trying to catch them. But, just as they're about to be caught, the demons pull some trickery. Move the lower half of the paper down and to the left, as in the second picture, and tell your friend to count the demons again. One of them has disappeared!

Rule the lines carefully on a piece of paper and then cut the paper diagonally as shown by the dotted line in the first picture. The trick is an eye fooler, and the disappearance of the tenth "demon" is an optical illusion. When you move the lower half of the paper, the remaining lines become a little longer than they were in the original position. The "disappearing" tenth line was equal in length to the total added length of the remaining lines.

THE CURSE OF THE SHIFTY EYES

HERE'S THE TRICK

You have special powers given to you by Martha Witch. She has taught you how to spot the "curse of the shifty eyes." Here's how to demonstrate your remarkable power:

Spread a deck of cards face down in your hand. Ask a friend to choose one carefully, look at it, memorize it and put it back anywhere in the deck. Cut the deck several times.

Now, pass the cards one by one before your friend's eyes. Be sure to tell him not to blink or move his eyes when he sees the card he picked. But no matter how steady his eyes are, you will know immediately when he sees his card—because of your special ability to spot his "curse of the shifty eyes"!

For this trick you have to use a deck of cards that has a picture or initials on the back, rather than an overall design which looks the same right side up or upside down.

1.   Before you begin the trick, secretly arrange the deck so that the pictures or initials on the backs of all the cards are right side up.

2.   While your friend is looking at his chosen card, hold the deck sideways in both hands.

3.   When your friend returns the card he picked, turn the deck so that his card is "upside down." Now all you have to do is look for the card with its back upside down when you pass the cards before his eyes.

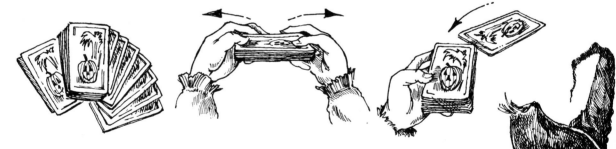

P.S. Poor Martha Witch. She can't use the cards with her initials to do this trick. Her initials are the same upside up and upside down!

THE TRUTH DETECTOR

HERE'S THE TRICK

Say to a friend, "Back in the old days, before there were lie detectors, Merlin the Wizard invented a *truth* detector. The truth detector measured the way people's voices changed when they told the truth."

Ask your friend if he thinks he can keep his voice steady while you show how the truth detector works. Hand him a deck of cards *face down* and tell him to choose a card from the middle of any pile, look at it and put it on top of any other pile. Tell him to stack the piles on top of each other, and then to cut the deck one time.

Now tell him to deal the cards, face up, one at a time, and to call the name of each card as he deals it. (Four of hearts, ace of diamonds.) Tell him to be very careful not to let his voice change when he calls the card he chose. But no matter how steady his voice is, you will be able to tell when he calls his card.

HERE'S HOW

1.   Prepare the deck ahead of time so that all four 4's are on top when the deck is face down and all four 10's are on the bottom.

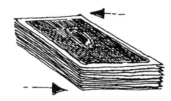

2.   Have your friend deal the cards out face down, in four equal piles, and select a card from the *middle* of one pile and put it on top of another pile. There will be a 10 on top of each pile and a 4 on the bottom.

3. So, even after he cuts the deck one time, and stacks the piles together, the card he has selected will be *between* a 4 and a 10. All the other 4's will be *next* to 10's.

NOTE: You don't even have to watch him deal the cards. Just listen carefully. Whenever he calls a 4 and then a card that isn't a 10, or a 10 and then a card that isn't a 4, *that*'s his card. To make the trick even more amazing, let your friend call out several more cards before you tell him what the chosen card was. (Have another deck of cards prepared in case he wants a repeat of the trick. Or tell him that you never repeat.)

CREEPY FELIPE

HERE'S THE TRICK

Tell this story to your friends: "Many years ago, there was a hangman called Felipe (say Fah-Leep-ee). He used to hang giant bandits who roamed the land.

"The giants hated Felipe and tried to destroy him. But Felipe met a witch who cast her magic spell on him and on his rope, which she called *Creepy Felipe*. So, no matter how often the bandits chopped the rope into pieces, Creepy Felipe always managed to pull himself together—just when hanging time came. Now, wonder of wonders, I have come into possession of that magic spell and I will show how it works."

Hold up a long piece of string (see Here's How). Then make a loop, and ask a friend to cut it with a pair of scissors. "Let's see if we can patch Creepy Felipe up again," you say.

Tie a knot and ask your friend to pull on one end of the string while you pull on the other to make the knot tight. Then take the string back and say some magic words as you pass your hand along its entire length. The knot disappears and Creepy Felipe is one long string again!

HERE'S HOW

1. Before you do this trick, tie a small piece of string (about 5 inches long) in a single knot to the center of the long string (about 2 feet long), so that one end of the small string is 4 inches long. Hide the knot and short piece in your hand by holding up the long string while clutching it over the sliding knot in the middle.

2. Now bring your hands together and pretend to hold up a loop from the center of the string. Actually, you make a loop from the longer end of the small string. It is this loop that your friend cuts. (He *thinks* he is cutting "Creepy Felipe" in two, but he's really only cutting off the small piece.)

3. Now, tie another knot with the two small ends, hiding in one hand the end of the small string that's been cut off. (You can slip the piece into your pocket while sniffing and trying to find a handkerchief.) Now you can show the "knotted" string freely. Give one end of the long string to your friend while you hold the other end. Tell him to pull the knot tight.

4. Now, with one hand, take the end of the long string that your friend was holding and quickly pass your other hand along the entire length of the string saying, "Zing, Pling, Araka ying. From two pieces make one string." As you do this, hold the knot loosely between your thumb and your closed fingers, and the

knot will slide easily down and off. Wave the long string and hand it to your friends. While they are examining it, secretly hide the knot in your pocket.

HINT: Practice this trick before a mirror so you can perform it smoothly when you show it to friends.

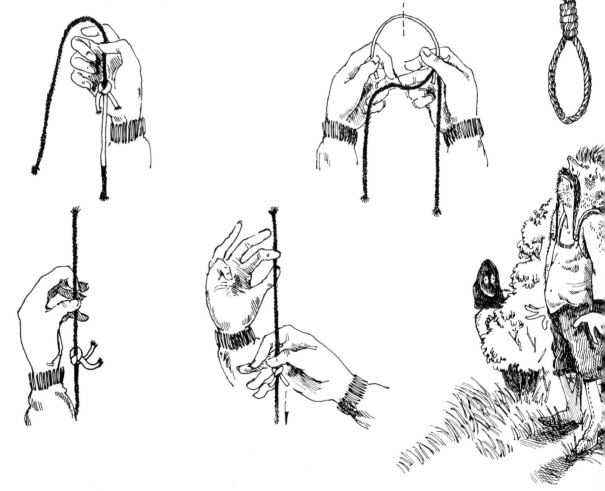

THE MAGIC SPOT

HERE'S THE TRICK

Tell your friends that when Wab the Wizard marks someone for a charmed life, he hands him the MAGIC SPOT. Ask if someone will be Wab's helper by handing out the MAGIC SPOT today.

Take a sheet of blank paper. Fold it in three sections across, and in three sections up and down. Then tear it along the folds into nine pieces of roughly the same size. Next, pass out the nine pieces of paper, giving the center piece to Wab's helper, who is to deliver the MAGIC SPOT. Tell him to make a mark on his paper. Gather the papers in a hat or box and explain that the MAGIC SPOT is so powerful you can *feel* its vibrations. Ask someone to blindfold you. Then stir the papers with your hand for a moment. Pull out—presto!— the MAGIC SPOT!

41

HERE'S HOW

As the drawing shows, all the pieces of paper will have at least one even edge except for the center piece which has torn edges all around. So, when you pass out the pieces of paper to your friends, just make sure that you give the center piece to your friend who is to deliver (mark) the MAGIC SPOT. You can easily feel this piece in the hat or box, because it has torn edges all around.

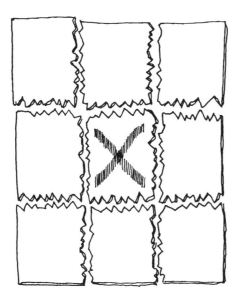

DRACULA'S PENCIL

HERE'S THE TRICK

Take a well-sharpened pencil and say to a group of friends: "This pencil was made from the very stake driven through the heart of Dracula. With the power from Dracula's Pencil, I can tell what goes on in other people's hearts and minds."

Ask a friend to call out two numbers between 1 and 9. Let's say he calls out numbers 4 and 7. Hand a book and Dracula's Pencil to a second friend. Ask him to turn to Chapter 4 and to lightly circle the seventh word.

Next, take an envelope from your pocket, put Dracula's Pencil inside it and seal it closed. Hold the envelope to your ear for a moment and then—abracadabra—announce the word your friend has circled.

You need nine specially-prepared-in-advance envelopes, and a book with at least nine chapters. Wear clothes with at least three large pockets, for completely hiding the envelopes. On the inside flap of envelope 1, write down the first nine words of Chapter 1 of the book. On the inside flap of envelope 2, write down the first nine words of Chapter 2. Do the same thing for the rest of the envelopes and hide them ahead of time as shown in the diagram.

1.   Put envelopes 1, 2, and 3 in one pocket (1 closest to your body, 3 farthest away); envelopes 4, 5, and 6 in another pocket (4 nearest you); and envelopes 7, 8, and 9 in the third pocket (with 7 closest to you).

2.   When your friend calls out numbers 4 and 7 and while your other friend is turning to the fourth chapter to circle the seventh word, take envelope 4 out of its pocket. Glance at the flap and remember the seventh word.

3. After sealing Dracula's Pencil in the envelope, hold it to your ear. Look mysterious. Then announce the circled word and let your friends marvel at your magic powers.

STORIES

THE VELVET RIBBON

Once there was a man who fell in love with a beautiful girl. And before the next full moon rose in the sky, they were wed.

To please her husband, the young wife wore a different gown each night. Sometimes she was dressed in yellow; other nights she wore red or blue or white. And she always wore a black velvet ribbon around her slender neck.

Day and night she wore that ribbon, and it was not long before her husband's curiosity got the better of him.

"Why do you always wear that ribbon?" he asked.

She smiled a strange smile and said not a word.

At last her husband got angry. And one night he shouted at his bride. "Take that ribbon off! I'm tired of looking at it."

"You will be sorry if I do," she replied, "so I won't."

Every morning at breakfast, the husband ordered his wife to remove the black velvet ribbon from around her neck. Every night at dinner he told her the same thing.

But every morning at breakfast and every night at dinner, all his wife would say was, "You'll be sorry if I do. So I won't."

46

A week passed. The husband no longer looked into his wife's eyes. He could only stare at that black velvet ribbon around her neck.

One night as his wife lay sleeping, he tiptoed to her sewing basket. He took out a pair of scissors.

Quickly and quietly, careful not to awaken her, he bent over his wife's bed   and
SNIP! went the scissors, and velvet ribbon fell to the floor
                              and
SNAP! off came her head. It rolled over the floor in the moon-light, wailing tearfully:

   "I . . . told . . . you . . . you'd . . . be . . . s-o-r-r-y!"

THE PEELING WALLPAPER

Martha hired a driver to take her to a small cottage in the country, where she would stay while her city apartment was being painted. The cottage stood alone, high on a cliff.

It was a bleak and lonely place and Martha was glad she would only be there for a few days. She told the driver when to return for her and watched him drive away, feeling suddenly alone and frightened.

Though it was summer, the cottage felt cold and damp, and Martha lit a fire in the fireplace. Then she looked around at the room. The few pieces of furniture were shabby, but the wall, covered with stained and peeling green wallpaper was even shabbier.

Martha stared at the wall. Something seemed horribly wrong with it. Then she gasped. *She could see right through it.* There stood a murky forest, and weaving among the trees were figures —dancing, creeping and waving their arms.

The scene disappeared as quickly as it had come. Martha tried to tell herself that what she had seen was only shadows from the fire. But when she looked at the wall again, she saw

that the wallpaper had peeled even more, leaving great, gaping holes.

That night Martha could not sleep. The wind blew strong and the flames danced eerily in the fireplace.

There they were again! Those creatures—*through the wall*—closer now, creeping and moving their arms, beckoning to her. Martha watched in horror as they formed a circle and began a slow dance. The wind blew harder and it seemed to Martha that she heard a crying and a wailing: "We will meet very soon, Martha. We are coming for you."

Martha fell asleep at last, dreaming of creatures creeping and wailing in the moonlight of a murky forest. The next morning, Martha saw that great strips of the wallpaper hung down in tatters.

Martha stayed outside all day, but when darkness fell, she came in and lit a fire in the room that seemed even colder than it had been before.

As the flames crept higher, the wall seemed to come alive with moving, creeping figures, crying: "We will meet very soon, Martha. We are coming for you."

Martha got into bed, closed her eyes tight and covered her ears. But still she saw the creatures creeping closer and closer. Still she heard their chants—louder and louder.

Martha huddled under the covers. She had never been so cold. She tried not to think of the wall with its moving, chanting creatures. Instead she forced herself to think of her cozy apartment in the city, freshly painted and cheerful.

Martha stole a quick look at the wall. The wallpaper was now in shreds. The creatures were still there—so close she could see their gray faces, with their glinty eyes, twisted mouths and crooked teeth.

A crackling sound made Martha jump. Had a log snapped in the fire? No—an arm—a creature's arm—was coming through the wall! "Please—oh please—let morning come," she moaned.

The night seemed endless and the wails and chants never ceased. Once she thought she felt something go tap, tap on her shoulder.

At last it was morning. Soon the car came and Martha was driven back to the city.

In front of her building, she paid the driver and ran up the stairs to her apartment. She opened the door and stood frozen to the spot.

There they were! The creatures! Dozens of them—creeping, moving toward her, waving their arms. Just before she fainted dead away, Martha saw them reach up and rip masks away from their faces.

There stood her friends, laughing as they chanted: "We have come for you, Martha. We have come for your birthday. Surprise!"

THE DINNER PARTY

She was late for the dinner party. By the time she got there, the guests had already started to eat. The hostess led her to her seat, next to a young man.

She was an artist and he was a writer and the two of them discovered that they had many things to talk about. Indeed, they were so busy talking that they stayed at the table, long after the other guests had moved to the living room.

The writer said, "I'd like to tell you what happened today when I sat down to write." He began whispering, though no one else was in the room to hear. "Have you ever had the feeling," he went on, "that you have lost all control of your work—almost as if a powerful, supernatural force was making you do something you didn't want to do? This morning I began writing a story about . . ."

"How strange," said the artist, interrupting him. "But this very same thing happened to me today. For a long time I've wanted to draw the scene outside of my window, and I was planning to work on that today. But what I drew was something so different—something I've never even thought about before. It was just as you said—some powerful force was leading my hand, controlling the picture."

"What was the picture?" asked the writer, leaning forward intently.

"A man being led to the electric chair," said the artist. "For murder, I guess. But the strangest thing about the picture was that the murderer was a cripple—one leg was much shorter than the other." The artist paused, remembering. Then she said, "But I'm sorry. You were about to tell me your experience when I interrupted you."

But the writer suddenly seemed very upset. His fingers moved

restlessly among the forks and knives still left on the table.

"My story, yes. Well, as you know," he said, "I write nature tales, mostly about animals. But this morning I wrote something so foreign to me, so hideous. A story of a man who commits murder—for no reason whatsoever."

Suddenly the writer got up from the table; his hand was clutching a knife. And as he limped toward the artist, she could see that one leg was much shorter than the other. . . . . .

A FISHING TRIP

The time Peter and Jim decided to go fishing was the time of the year when darkness comes without warning, when shadows make strange shapes in the trees, and when the creatures of the forest hoot and shriek all night long. It was the time of Halloween.

Peter and Jim stumbled upon a lake neither had ever been to before. The fishing was good and they were in no hurry to get home. They fished until the last light had left the sky. There was no moon and the way was strange. There were no signs, no houses to stop at for directions. The more they walked, the more lost they became.

Soon they were deep in the woods. As soon as Peter and Jim lit a match to see their way, it went out. A wind came up, and the trees' branches swayed and rasped like bony fingers. Suddenly a wide patch appeared before them, leading to an old, dark house. It was set in a grove of dead trees, laced with spider webs. Smoke came from the chimneys of the house, and the two boys sniffed the delicious smell of something baking.

"Someone lives here," said Peter. "They'll tell us how to get home."

The two boys knocked. The heavy door slowly swung open. Inside a candle flame flickered and went out. There was the sound of something falling, and then silence.

Though Jim and Peter had seen smoke pouring from the chimneys, they saw no fires in the fireplaces. Though they had smelled the delicious smell of baking, the house was cold and musty-smelling. There was no sign of life anywhere.

"This place gives me the creeps," said Peter. "Let's go."

"I don't know why," said Jim, "but I just remembered a story the men tell, about a haunted house north of a lake. Most of the year, they say, the house stands empty. It's so spooky that even the spirits stay away!

"But once a year, on Halloween, the spirits all meet there to add a new member to their group. Isn't that silly, Peter? No one knows how they get their new members. It's still a mystery. Sound like nonsense, right, Peter? Haunted houses and spirits and . . . . Peter? Peter? Peter? PETER!"

POEM/GAME

THE TERRIBLE TALKY NOT-QUITE

This is the most terrible poem ever written. The poet could not get up the nerve to finish some rhymes. Won't you and your friends help the poor poet by filling in the blanks?

You won't ever know such a fright,
Till you wake in the dark of the _____,
    And find on the floor
    Where there was none before,
A terrible talky Not-Quite.

A Not-Quite must talk all the time,
And most of its words are in _____,
    To say which is worse,
    Its looks or its verse,
Would take more of a brain than I'm.

"You'll pardon me if I don't sit.
I'm afraid if I do I might split.
        When they sewed up my _____,
        They used two different teams,
And somehow I've never quite fit."

"You'll find I don't like to stand,
Because my left foot is a _____,
        And that being so,
        I wear on my big toe,
A Not-Quite real gold wedding band."

"We Not-Quites do not really care,
That we have neither feathers nor _____,
        For we all have concurred,
        That we're handsomely furred,
Which is better than being quite bare."

"Have you ever touched flesh slick and slimy,
And covered with bumps soiled and grimy?
        Well, that is what grows,
        From my shins to my _____,
So if that's what you like, why not try me?"

"Of course, I don't mind that I've scales,
Where other Not-Quites have toenails.
　　But I'd be such a cutie,
　　Except that my _____,
Is spoiled by these holes in my tails."

"Do you think I'm as mad as a hatter?
If you don't, then what is the matter?
　　Though it's not even dawn,
　　You keep stifling a _____,
I hope you're not bored with my chatter."

"Well, I've several more calls I must make,
There's a party with ice cream and _____.
　　And at quarter past three,
　　I'm invited to tea,
Then at four there's our yearly clambake."

"It's really too bad I can't _____."
Said the Not-Quite, while trying to skate.
　　Then the hideous THING,
　　Cranked up its back wing,
And promised to fly back by eight.

DIABOLICAL SKIT

It's fun to put on a skit. You'll need a few props for Dr. Diabolical's office—a telephone and a telescope for examining patients. (If you don't have a telescope, take an empty cardboard tube from a role of paper towels and paint it black.)

Make costumes that suit the characters.

For spooky sound effects, blow over an empty bottle or shake a jar of pebbles or nuts.

And here are plenty of jokes to liven your act.

62

A DAFFY DAY AT DOCTOR DIABOLICAL'S OFFICE

Dr. Diabolical (on the telephone): No, no, madam! Don't give
    your baby elephant milk!

Voice (offstage): Why not? I'm his mother and I'm an elephant!
    (*Dr. Diabolical hangs up.*)

    (*Mrs. Witch runs in, frantic.*)

Mrs. Witch: Willy fell into the river. What is the first thing he
    should do?

Dr. Diabolical (with an evil grin): Get wet, of course.

Mrs. Witch: Willy can't sleep at night. What shall he do?

Dr. Diabolical: Tell him to sleep near the edge of the bed. He'll
    drop off more easily. And, as for you, I think you need a
    long rest.

Mrs. Witch: But you haven't even examined me. Why don't you
    look at my tongue?

Dr. Diabolical: I don't have to. I'm sure it could use a long rest,
    too. Next patient, please!

(*Mrs. Vampire enters, with her daughter Velma.*)

Mrs. Vampire: I'm worried about Velma.

Dr. Diabolical: What seems to be the matter?

Mrs. Vampire: She's lost her appetite. Now she won't eat any-
body.

Velma Vampire: And what's more, I can't do my homework.

Dr. Diabolical (frowning): What does losing your appetite have
to do with your homework?

Velma Vampire: How can I write on an empty stomach?

Dr. Diabolical: Have you tried writing on a piece of paper?

(*Enter old Mr. Ghoul.*)

Mr. Ghoul: I've got a pain in my leg.

Dr. Diabolical: There's nothing I can give you for it. It's old age.

Mr. Ghoul: But, doctor, the left leg is just as old as the right one
and it doesn't hurt at all. And I've got another problem. I
keep eating strawberries.

Dr. Diabolical: What's the matter with that? I eat strawberries
every chance I get.

Mr. Ghoul: Off the wallpaper?

(*Daffy Demon enters, his clothes in rags.*)

Daffy Demon: Help me! I just ate a stick of dynamite!

Dr. Diabolical: Why did you do that silly thing?

Daffy Demon: I wanted my hair to grow out in bangs.

Dr. Diabolical (examining him): Hmmm. I see that you have little white things in your head that bite.

Daffy Demon (in alarm): What are they, doctor?

Dr. Diabolical: Your teeth!

(*Sam Skeleton comes in.*)

Sam Skeleton: I'm so thin, doctor. What is the best way to get fat?

Dr. Diabolical: Go to the butcher shop! On your way out, tell my nurse to come in, please.

Nurse (offstage): I can't come now, doctor.

Dr. Diabolical: Why not?

Nurse: I made myself some tea and I swallowed my teaspoon, so now I can't stir. Griselda Ghost is on her way in.

66

(*Enter Griselda Ghost.*)

Griselda Ghost: You must help me, doctor. I can't seem to remember anything I've just said.

Dr. Diabolical: That sounds serious. When did you first notice
this problem?

Griselda Ghost: What problem?

(*Phone rings, Dr. Diabolical answers it.*)

Dr. Diabolical: Doctor speaking.

Watery Voice (offstage): Help me, doctor. A ghoul just bit off
my arm!

Dr. Diabolical: Which one?

Watery Voice: How should I know? All eight of them look alike.
(*Doctor throws down the phone.*)

(*Horrible Monster enters.*)

Horrible Monster: Quick! Give me something to cure hiccups.
(Dr. Diabolical slaps him hard on the back.)

Horrible Monster: Why did you do that?

Dr. Diabolical (pleased with himself): Well, you don't have
hiccups anymore, do you?

Horrible Monster: I never did. It's my brother who has them.
Give me something to scare him with!

Dr. Diabolical: Just smile at him.

(*Enter Winnie Witch.*)

Winnie Witch: Oh, I feel terrible.

Dr. Diabolical: What's the matter?

Winnie Witch: Thousands of invisible bugs are crawling all
over me!

Dr. Diabolical (*grabbing his hat and running out*): Well, don't
brush them off on me!